The New Leader

CONGRATULATIONS ON YOUR PROMOTION! NOW WHAT?

ROBERT L. BAILEY

AUTHOR OF
PLAIN TALK ABOUT LEADERSHIP

the Peppertree Press
Sarasota, Florida

CONTENTS

Promotions are one of life's most challenging times, even ahead of death of a family member, divorce, moving and managing teenage children.

Here are the steps you should take on your first few days and weeks on the job.

This simple but critically important principle drives all effective leadership, but too many leaders overlook it.

Most leaders fail because they are unwilling to pay the price that good leadership requires.

DEDICATION

Over the course of my career, perhaps a half dozen people—in addition to my parents, my spouse and my family—have had the greatest influence on my life and my career. One such individual is Tom Mayhew.

Tom was my first "real boss." Yes, I had many other bosses—when I was a kid working on our family farm, when I was working a night job on the Frisco Railroad to finance my college education, and when I was in the military. But Tom was my first real boss as I set out on my career in the property and casualty insurance industry.

When I joined his company in 1958, he was a vice president—and he later became president—of the Western Casualty and Surety Company of Fort Scott, Kansas, a company that has since virtually disappeared as it was absorbed into a new parent, and as the new parent was absorbed into still another parent. In the quest for bigness in this merger and acquisition world, some truly excellent companies have evaporated.

I learned more from Tom about the property and casualty insurance business than any other single individual. He gave me an opportunity to grow—to take on new challenges—to spread my wings—to be exposed to nearly every phase of the business. He guided, tutored, corrected, pushed and prodded, with more patience than I deserved. Apparently he saw something in me that I did not see in myself.

Tom's guidance and influence amounted to a relatively effective jump-start in the property and casualty insurance business—a business that has treated the Bailey family pretty well. It was his guidance and influence, along with the principles of the "old Western," that shaped my business philosophies as I began my journey in the business world and that ultimately helped us build a sizable and very successful property and casualty insurance company group—the State Auto Insurance Companies—which I led for many years. In every respect we tried to reflect those principles—where a person's word is as good as any contract—where every person is treated as you or I would want to be treated. It's a formula that spells success every time.

This book is dedicated to the memory of Tom—my first real boss, my mentor, my friend—for he was responsible for giving me a solid footing in an industry that I grew to love and for giving me the firm shove I needed to achieve a reasonable degree of success in the business world.

* * * * *

After preparing the manuscript for this book, but before its publication, Tom died at the age of 87. Learning of his ill health several weeks before his death, I emailed a copy of this dedication to him through his son, Rick. At the time of his death, Rick told me that these pages were near the top of his reading stack next to his favorite chair.

When I see Tom again, I plan to express my thanks and appreciation to him in person.

Robert L. Bailey

ACKNOWLEDGMENTS

There are so many people who deserve my thanks and appreciation that I know any list I might compile will fall short. Here are just a few who merit acknowledgment:

Lane Gutstein, my editor.
Lane is a former English teacher, a lover of books, and a writing expert. She made many suggestions to correct and improve this book. Unfortunately, the book writing process never ends until the press rolls. I continued to add, delete, and make changes (and errors) while Lane was editing the last rewrite. The errors that remain are my own.

Editor-in-Chief Tom McCoy
of *Rough Notes* magazine,
one of the nation's leading insurance industry publications (see www.roughnotes. com). Since 2002 *Rough Notes* has carried my column "Lessons in Leadership". In each column I try to make a point that is important

to our business readers and drive it home with stories and illustrations, usually drawn from some 40 plus years of business experience. Many of those stories have found their way into this book. Thank you, Tom, for allowing me to recycle some of that material.

Julie Ann Howell and **Teri Franco**,
of **Peppertree Press**,
and Graphic Designer **Elizabeth Peters**.

These folks turned a plain, unadorned manuscript into a pretty neat book. And unlike so many publishers who give the impression they're participating in a WWE SmackDown, they are a delight to work with. They took the pain out of the most difficult phase of bringing a book to market.

Perhaps I'm most indebted to the many folks I've worked with through the years. There are far too many to list. I can think of hundreds from whom I've learned something that has contributed to my understanding of business and leadership and has made a positive impact on my life. To all of you, I say "thanks."

INTRODUCTION

Your dream has come true. You have achieved one of your life's most cherished goals. You have been promoted. You are now a leader and a member of management.

You call your spouse with the good news. When you arrive home your spouse has arranged a special celebration—your favorite meal, with candlelight and all the fancy trimmings. Your kids share in your excitement with hugs and kisses, and parents and close friends express their happiness for you in congratulatory phone calls.

The thrill of your achievement begins to wane by bedtime. You toss and turn throughout the night as you think about the realities of the challenges ahead. What if I lead aggressively—and I look around and no one is following? What if I am resented by my new subordinates, many of whom believe that they should have been the ones promoted? What if I fail as a leader because I am unable to get the results expected by senior management?

A million similar questions dash through your mind throughout the restless night. By morning the thrill of achievement has faded and you have begun to believe that you don't have what it takes to be a successful leader.

If it's any consolation, you should know that these thoughts raid the minds of many new leaders. Nearly one in five say "promotions" are one of life's most challenging times, even ahead of death of a family member, divorce, moving, and managing teenage children.

Without question, leadership is a difficult and sometimes terrifying job, under even the best of circumstances. Performing a job and leading others require entirely different skill sets.

Learning critical leadership skills is complicated by so many pathetic role models in leadership positions in our country. Movies and television nearly always depict the leader as a worthless, self-centered goofus. Of the some 150 million employed people in America, some surveys tell us that as many as 72% don't like their jobs or their bosses. Some 50% of American workers have already checked out mentally in that they say they are actively seeking another job right now or say they would accept one if an opportunity presented itself. This is not a badge of honor for American business leaders, but unfortunately it's true.

The picture is not improved by those in the most visible leadership roles in our country—politicians. Too many American politicians give the impression that they are interested in only three things—raising money, getting elected, and getting re-elected—as they go about their business of playing a highly publicized game of "gotcha." Their voracious quest for the power and perks of elected office give the impression that their actions are all about "me," the politician, without regard to "you" or your interests as constituents. There is little in the field of politics that great leaders should emulate.

The cost of poor leadership is overwhelming. Gallop estimates that 70% of American workers are "disengaged." And Gallop further estimates that these disengaged workers are costing American businesses some $300 billion a year.

It's difficult for most of us to relate to numbers that range into the billions, so let's break that down to your own company or department. Start with the annual payroll of your company or the department for which you are responsible. Take 70% of that total payroll to determine the payroll of those employees who might be categorized as "disengaged."

Now, how much slippage are you getting? That is, how much less effective is the disengaged worker compared to the individual who is fully committed to doing a great job for your company and its customers? Let's say that's 50%. Obviously 50% of 70% (or 35% of your total payroll) is a lot of money and may well mean the difference between a successful company and a failing company.

But there are other costs that must be added. For most companies we consistently estimate that there is a full dollar of overhead for every dollar of payroll: 30% or 40% for benefits; a desk or work station; equipment they work with, such as a PC or telephone; a parking place; for every 15 or 20 people, there's another supervisor; etc.

This takes you back to a full 70% of your payroll that perhaps is being flushed down the drain every payday because workers are disengaged.

That's a lot of money. And that doesn't count the loss of business created by uncaring, disengaged employees. Customers who experience poor service often leave, and they tell others about the unacceptable service they received. It's difficult to document precisely what this costs, but it's an astounding number.

Although there are exceptions, I believe that most of these costs are the result of poor leadership.

I'm convinced that it need not be that way. I believe strongly that you can build a productive, energized, committed, gung-ho, high morale workforce. The process is not fast, and it's not easy. But it's not rocket science either. You are smart; you work hard; and you have the ability to get results or you would not have been given this opportunity to lead. You have the wherewithal to become an outstanding leader.

A question often asked is, "Are leaders born? Or are they made?" For more than 40 years I have observed many leaders at work, and I'm convinced they are made.

You too can become a truly outstanding leader by applying the principles you will learn in this book.

Are you ready? Let's get started.

1

SHOULD I HIT THE GROUND RUNNING?

It's your first day on the job, and you've been wrestling with this question for days, even weeks. "Should I hit the ground running?"

Should I impress my new subordinates with my knowledge of the industry? Should I demonstrate to them that I'm a person of action—a "get it done" no nonsense kind of individual? Should I let them know in no uncertain terms that they'd better jump on board or prepare to get run over? Should I throw a scare into them like a junior high teacher on the first day of school?

In most cases I recommend that you not hit the ground running.

It should be no surprise that you're not going to be able to operate your business, or your department, alone. Many leaders forget this, even seasoned ones. You need a team of capable people to pull it off.

Members of that team know more about their specific areas of the organization than you can possibly know. They can help you win—or they can almost certainly guarantee your failure. My advice is to cash in on their knowledge and win their support.

As a first step, I recommend that you meet with your direct reports (or in a smaller organization, with all your employees), so they can know what you look like and can see a little slice of your personality. This is not a problem-solving meeting. It's a get-acquainted meeting, a very preliminary team-building meeting. You can ask for questions, but don't expect many—probably none. At this point nobody knows whether or not the messenger will get shot, so most won't take the chance. You can be assured that they will be suspicious of your motives.

Meetings like this can be painful. I can recall meeting with employees located in outlying offices when I became president of my former company. Most sat with their arms folded. Every eye seemed to say, *"I don't know you. I don't trust you. I don't like you. I know you're not having this meeting for the fun of it. You have bad news to give us today. I know you're closing the office. You're pulling out of the state. I know I'm being terminated. We're all losing our jobs. Stop the BS and get on with it."*

Negative assumptions like this are normal, for I found that most employees of our company (and perhaps your company too) had never been invited to meetings of this nature unless there was bad news. Yes, unfortunately that's a sad commentary for American business.

You, their new leader, must break down these underlying beliefs and start building a new open, communicative corporate culture. This will require time. In my former company, I met monthly with home office people and every three or four months with employees in outlying offices, and I found that communication barriers were still being broken down three years later.

Tell them in that first meeting that we have many challenges ahead. Name two or three of them, no matter how sensitive. They already know what they are, and they'll build just a tad of respect for you by your willingness to acknowledge some of the problems the organization is facing. Tell them that you need their help in finding appropriate solutions and in bringing about success and prosperity for the company and security and opportunities for its people.

Remember, they're probably expecting bad news today. Don't expect to accomplish too much.

This is your pre-game pep talk. Stay positive and optimistic. But don't lie. They're going to remember what you said, and they will expect subsequent messages, goals and objectives, for both the short term and long term, to be consistent with what you said today. This is only the first of many such communications.

Tell them that you'll be meeting with them one-on-one to get their ideas and suggestions for building a great company.

Chances are they won't believe you. They think you are going to do what you want to do and that their suggestions will not be welcomed.

So follow through. You will pleasantly surprise them when you do.

Consider beginning these one-on-one meetings something like this: "*It will be no surprise* to you that we have some giant challenges that we have to tackle if we are to survive and prosper as a company and if we are to provide security and opportunities for our people. As CEO (or manager, supervisor, etc.), I've been asked to lead this effort. But I need your help. You've been around longer than I have (or you know this department or specific area better than I do), so your perspective is invaluable. If you were the CEO (or manager) instead of me, what would be the top five things you would do to meet our business objectives?"

Now sit back. Listen. And listen.

Make notes. Even if you can remember what was said, it's critical that you let your people know that what they say is important to you—important enough that you wrote it down. Ask questions only to draw out the subordinate. Take no exceptions to anything that is said. Just make notes—and listen.

If this has been a non-communicative company or department in the past (and too many have been), this process will begin slowly. Many will be trying to figure out, "Does he or she really want to know? Will I get in trouble if I express my views?" Several meetings like this over a period of weeks may be required to get substantive information.

5

When interviews with all your people are completed, chances are you'll see consistency in what was recommended.   And chances are that the list of action items they have suggested are consistent with the ideas you had in mind all along. It's a confirmation of what you believed but were not close enough to the company or department to know for sure. When several make the same suggestion, much of the risk inherent with any decision is removed.

Bring together again your direct reports (or all your people in a smaller company) with the new action plan. "All of you have been asked to help get this company (or department) moving again, and you've come up with some great ideas. We're going to put several of your ideas to work right away. This is probably all we can digest right now. Other ideas will be put to work as soon as we can get our arms around a few of these high priority items."

Then name the top two, three or four things that will be put into effect now. Those in the room who have made these suggestions will be thrilled that you actually listened. Most probably thought that you had not listened and that their ideas would never see the light of day.

6

That's called "buy in." Members of the team are not putting your ideas to work; they're putting their ideas to work.

Members of the group who had been fearful of making any suggestions are now beginning to recognize that you were sincere about asking for their input. "After all, those who made suggestions didn't get shot, so maybe I have nothing to fear," they will think.

Express thanks and appreciation in your next one-on-one meeting to those who made the suggestions that were adopted. It may not yet be appropriate to recognize them publicly, for some of their peers may badger them for "sucking up" to management. Don't put them into this position until most of their associates buy into this new open communication company where employee suggestions are valued.

Communication efforts like this are a continuing process. It's been my experience that one, two, three, even ten years from now, there's a new set of problems as significant as those being faced today. You'll need the suggestions of your people—and you'll need their commitment—years from now just as you do today.

Great companies are great for a reason. The people within the company must see it as their company, not your company. Employee passion that brings about great performance comes from that ownership. We'll be talking about the elements that bring about that commitment throughout this book.

As with any general rule, there are exceptions. Sometimes the new leader should hit the ground running. If the organization is experiencing serious financial problems—it is having difficulty meeting Friday's payroll— there may not be enough time for "buy in." In that case, tell your people in that initial meeting that two or three activities must take place immediately if this organization is to survive. Be specific. Then begin the fine-tuning process with your one-on-one meetings with your people as we have discussed.

By involving your people in identifying problems and possible solutions, you'll build a successful company—you'll build a stronger team—and you'll be well on your way to becoming a pretty darn good leader.

2

THE FOUNDATION OF LEADERSHIP

There's a simple principle that drives all effective leadership. When people are pushed, they tend to push back. You don't like to be pushed; I don't like to be pushed; and no one else I've ever met likes to be pushed. So effective leaders must learn how to encourage followers without pushing, for we know if we push, they will push back. This should be a fairly obvious truth in management circles, but sadly too many leaders have never figured it out.

Dwight D. Eisenhower, former President and General, once summarized this principle very well: *"You don't lead by hitting people over the head. That's assault, not leadership."*

I should point out that in this overall field of management, one phase of which is

9

leadership, sometimes people have to be pushed. There are times when a person cannot perform, will not perform, has an agenda that is inconsistent with that of the organization, and, therefore, has to be pushed—or disciplined—and sometimes fired. That's not leadership, but it's definitely a part of the management process.

If an employee shows up for work drunk, you will probably have to fire him or her. Or if a worker steals from the company, termination is in order. When it comes to integrity, I recommend a zero tolerance policy. If an employee will cheat the company out of $5, there is little doubt what he or she will do when the bounty is $5,000 or $150,000.

Therefore, in your job as a manager, periodically you may have to push—or reprimand—or even fire. But if you have to do it very often—say more than one or two employees out of a hundred—something is desperately wrong. Likely the selection process wasn't thorough enough. We'll cover the practice of hiring high quality people later.

For the vast majority of workers, we need to figure out how to motivate and encourage their high performance and commitment to the company and its customers without our pushing them, for we know if we push them, they will push back.

Leadership has many dimensions. Thousands of college courses are available in this field, and one can study the topic for many years. I certainly don't want to demean the study of leadership by oversimplification. Still, I believe that every single dimension of leadership can be summed up with one word. That word is communication. Every aspect of leadership requires good, thorough, effective, ongoing communication.

Great leaders tend to be great communicators.

I challenge you to name a truly great leader who is not a truly great communicator.

Communication is important because your people sincerely want to know what's going on in the company. What competitive challenges are being faced by the company? Is the company gaining on the competition or is it losing the competitive battle? What is being done to solve some of the serious problems that are so highly publicized in the trade press? Your people want to know.

- - - - - Robert L. Bailey - - - - -

Perhaps there are far too many sports analogies in business. Yet the loyalty, commitment and enthusiasm of winning companies compare to that of winning sports teams.

I love college football especially. There is nothing more exciting than a Saturday afternoon watching a favorite college football team in action. Bands, cheer leaders, and a hundred thousand screaming fans bring the enthusiasm level to a fever pitch.

There's just one thing I don't like about college football. I believe the scoring system is sometimes unfair. Too often one team has more yards rushing, more yards passing, more first downs, and it has possession of the ball for a longer period than the opposing team. It wins in every statistical category except one— the final score. It lost the game. I believe this is unfair.

Therefore, I am proposing a change in the way football is scored. My suggestion is that the scoreboard and the white lines be removed from the field. Instead, the officials will rate every player on every play in terms of the accuracy of passing, the precision in running the patterns, the effectiveness of the blocks and tackles, etc.

All this will be fed into a very sophisticated computer system. All the statistics will be analyzed, and the winner of the game will be announced in, say, four to six weeks—but certainly no later than 45 days after the end of the calendar quarter.

If college football were scored in this manner, would you still attend college football games? Would you watch it on TV? Would football players still be willing to play the game?

The answers to all these questions is, "*Probably not.*" So perhaps my idea is not as good as I first thought.

Yet this is exactly how most companies in America are operated. Few people know the score. Few know what it takes to win.

The reason the American people are in love with sports is that this is one of the few places in life in which they have fast feedback. They know the score. They know how much time is left in the game. They know what they have to do to win the game.

If people can get excited about the success of a football team by knowing the score and the details of the game, it stands to reason that employees can relate to the success of their company by knowing the score and the details of the game.

And they want to know now. The faster, the better.

Aren't there proprietary company secrets that can't be shared? Yes, a few. But I've found that there are very few. I told my former employees that there are two things we could not tell them. As a publicly owned corporation, we could not tell them the quarterly earnings per share until they were announced to the investment community at large. And if we were negotiating for the purchase of a company or a piece of property and operating under a non-disclosure agreement, we could not tell them. When such information was no longer confidential, they were assured that they would be among the first to know. Everyone seemed to understand the rules and I can't think of anyone who seemed upset in the least.

How should information be disseminated? Use nearly every communication technique known to mankind. You can come up with many methods of keeping your people informed, but here are a few communication devices we found effective:

- - - - - THE NEW LEADER - - - - -

Senior management met at 7:00 a.m. every Monday. There was a short agenda, and every attendee was asked to give an update of what was going on in his or her department. It was a time to hash-out problems that overlap departments. The meeting adjourned at 8:00 a.m.

The 7:00 a.m. Monday time slot was chosen for a couple of reasons: (1) Senior management travel schedules were less likely to conflict; (2) It was a symbol to others that senior management gets an early start every week.

Monthly in the home office and three or four times a year in outlying offices, we held President's Open Forums. Attendance was not mandatory, but most employees in the outlying offices attended. Because of the larger employee population in the home office, everyone could not attend, but there was generally a standing room crowd. The employee grapevine carried the message to many others, so we reached a good number of employees every month.

Periodically there was a gripe—usually a legitimate one. When a problem could be fixed, we did it immediately. On one occasion I was told of a tree in one of our parking lots that produced a berry that stained cars parked there. That very day our buildings and grounds manager and I visited the parking lot and found the tree. The next day it was removed.

For the most part, however, there were no gripes—just genuine interest in the company and its direction, how industry problems were being dealt with, how we intend to respond to the actions of our competitors, and similar weighty matters. Employees at all levels want to be a part of, and want to contribute to, a successful organization.

Every week I scheduled at least two hours touring one wing of the building—east wing fourth floor one week, west wing fourth floor the next week, etc. I talked to every employee who was at his or her work station and not on the phone.

When I asked, "*How ya' doing?*" the answer was generally as meaningless as my question. But when I asked about the specific duties of the employee, I got solid answers. They were pleased to tell me about their jobs. When I asked what we could do to make their jobs easier, or simplify the process to improve service to our customers, they often had worthwhile ideas. When I asked about customer complaints, they could describe them

16

and had ideas for improvement. Likewise they could explain the things we were doing that especially pleased customers.

Although this is perhaps somewhat of an exaggeration, I believe this weekly two-hour tour paid for my full annual salary by learning something we were doing that we should not be doing, or finding something we should be doing that we weren't doing.

However, I never ever took action without the involvement of the appropriate middle management people. On several occasions I was told, *"Don't tell my boss (the middle management person) that I told you about this."* I never ever got the employee in trouble with his or her immediate boss. I would go to the immediate manager or supervisor and say, *"Somewhere I heard that this problem exists. Would you please check it out, and then let's talk about a possible solution."*

These face-to-face communication efforts were supplemented by the more traditional and formal communication techniques, such as newsletters. We published a quarterly newsletter and a monthly management letter. When the intranet came along, we put the newsletter on line and updated it daily. One feature of the intranet was forum.bob through which employees companywide could ask questions, anonymously if they wished. All questions were answered—no screening.

And we had company-produced videotapes, which I don't necessarily recommend. Most Americans have become accustomed to professional video presentations on TV, and most members of senior management come through on video as rank amateurs.

The messages contained in all these forms of communication must always be consistent—always driving home the objectives of the company and providing every bit of information possible to make employees feel like owners.

If you are to become an outstanding leader, you must become an outstanding communicator.

3

WHY MOST LEADERS FAIL

Yes, most leaders fail. They fail, not because of the lack of some critical skill, but because they are unwilling to pay the price—to make the sacrifice—that good leadership requires.

Leaders must set a positive, appropriate example.

Too many do not set a proper example for others. Instead the majority of people in leadership roles feel they have earned the right to take advantage of every perk and privilege imaginable.

Hardly a week passes that I do not hear examples of failing leaders across the country, and in nearly every case it's because the leader does not set a positive example. I've found that Dilbert is alive and well in this country.

A man in San Antonio, Texas, told me by email that the big boss flew into San Antonio on the corporate jet, took a stretch limo to the office, a driver waited outside for nearly four hours while employee and management meetings were being held—to tell them that they had to reduce their expenses. Nobody believed him—and very likely no expense-reduction actions will occur voluntarily—because they considered the boss's expenses wasteful and extravagant.

Example is the most powerful form of communication.

An email from Des Moines, Iowa, told of a company's effort to encourage employees to get to work on time and work a full eight-hour shift, while senior officers showed up at 9:00 or 9:30, took 1½ hours for lunch, and left the office by 3:00 p.m. or so, especially during the months when it was warm enough to play golf.

I could list hundreds and probably thousands of examples in which leaders fail to set an appropriate example, but that's probably unnecessary. Undoubtedly you have seen many such examples in your own work experience.

Behavior on the job is always a reflection of the behavior of the boss. There are no exceptions. None.

Dr. Carl Menninger, the founder of the Menninger Clinic in Topeka, Kansas, one of the foremost psychiatric clinics in the nation, has said the human being is 90% reactive and only 10% intellectual. Because we're reactive, when people wave, we wave back. When people smile, we smile back. For the most part we react to those around us. And most certainly we react to leaders we admire and respect.

Setting an appropriate example not only inspires employees but also has a far-reaching effect on the bottom line. Several years ago I was traveling to a board meeting of our insurance company trade association. While changing planes in Chicago, I ran into a friend, the CEO of a competing insurer, who likewise was attending the board meeting. We chatted for a few minutes as we were waiting for our rows to be called. *"I thought some other members of the board might be on this flight,"* I said, *"but I haven't seen anybody."*

"Oh, yes," he responded. *"Several are on this flight,"* and he proceeded to name them.

"They're already on board. They're flying first class."

"That's interesting," I chuckled. *"Of those companies whose CEOs are on board, only your company and my company are profitable. And we're flying coach. The others are unprofitable and they're flying first class."*

I don't know the difference in cost between first class and coach on that particular flight, but I'm sure it was fairly inconsequential in the total scheme of things. But flying first class is just one small symbol of waste and extravagance that tends to permeate an organization. Each symbol of a lavish lifestyle tends to be emulated by people throughout the organization. Together these practices could easily spell the difference between success and failure.

It was not an accident that Bill Gates flew coach even after Microsoft had become a multi-billion dollar corporation.

Whatever behavior you expect from employees, the leader sets the pace. Leaders must follow the same rules as everybody else.

Leaders are on flex time—they flex in early and flex out late.

- - - - - THE NEW LEADER - - - - -

They fly coach, like everyone else.

They answer their own phones—and make their own calls.

They dress the way their customers expect them to dress.

They park in the North 40 like everyone else. No reserved parking spots.

They eat in the company cafeteria like everyone else. Another advantage is the cafeteria is a great place to pick up information that you should know. When I've sat down with a group of employees in the cafeteria, there have been times that I've paralyzed the conversation mid-syllable. But over time they got used to it and the fear subsided when they learned that they would not get into trouble. Then a comment was made periodically, *"Did you know that.......? Have you thought about.......?"* Some valuable information came from the rank-and-file associates.

If you want a compassionate organization, the leader is compassionate. If you want an ethical organization, the leader is ethical. If you want an efficient organization, the leader is efficient. If you want a customer-focused organization, the leader is customer focused.

That's how it works. Simple stuff. But most leaders are unwilling to pull it off.

4

IT'S MORE
THAN DELEGATION

An important characteristic of a good leader is the ability and willingness to delegate. A more popular term in recent years has been empowerment.

Certainly delegation and empowerment play a role in good management. But I'm convinced that some of the most poorly managed companies in America are run by executives who fervently "delegate" and "empower."

Delegation and empowerment cannot be effective unless every person in the organization understands the "rules of the road"—what makes the company tick. I call this the philosophical framework that every company operates within.

There are several ingredients of a corporate philosophical framework: a standard for the treatment of employees, customer service standards, product quality standards, the company's reputation in the community and the industry, ethical standards.

Can you name a company for which you would not want to work? I can, and I'm certain you can. Any number of companies have a reputation of treating employees poorly.

On the other hand, can you name a company that has a reputation of being a good place to work? Again, I can. And no doubt you can. Hopefully you named your own organization. These companies are known for caring about their people, paying competitive salary levels and providing good benefits.

Can you name companies with which you don't want to do business? Chances are there are several. I will drive a hundred miles if necessary to keep from doing business with some organizations. Their service is poor, work quality is shabby, and they have a reputation of ripping off customers whenever they have an opportunity.

And you can name companies with which you want to do business. They sell great products or services, and they go the extra mile to take care of their customers.

Companies in all these categories operate within a philosophical framework. It may have been established inadvertently or purposely. In either case, it casts a prominent shadow over every aspect of company operations. And in either case, it reflects the value system established by the leader who lives and breathes it.

What type of philosophical framework do you want to establish for your company or department?

If you are told by your superior, *"We want to make money here—and I don't care how you do it,"* just what kind of behavior is expected? How should you treat your employees? Should you attract good people with competitive salaries and benefits? Or should you employ warm bodies, keep salaries and benefits at the lowest possible level if these actions would enhance the goal to *"make money—and I don't care how you do it?"*

What type of service should be given to customers? Should you provide overwhelming service so that word-of-mouth marketing will work for you? Or should you let service levels deteriorate in order to keep overhead costs as low as possible and enhance the short-term profit picture?

What role should your organization play in your community and your industry? Should you contribute to worthwhile community causes? Or are you expected to remove the company from any cause that might cost money? Should you be concerned about your company's reputation in its industry?

What about ethical standards? Are you expected to steal a car from a competitor if it advances your company's cause to *"make money—and I don't care how you do it?"*

A successful company needs a consistent philosophical framework—a solid reputation of always treating employees and customers fairly; of consistently providing overwhelming customer service and selling products of the highest quality; of always conducting itself with the highest ethical standards.

Some companies intend to do the right thing but end up with inconsistent reputations. It's favorable in some areas of the country, unfavorable in others. One company may look like a totally different company in different parts of the country. This occurs because local managers have the discretion of building their own philosophical framework without companywide guidance.

The problem here is that reputations know no geographic bounds. Sooner or later an incident of poor service or unethical behavior will reach into other markets. It's a near certainty that a poor reputation in any market over time will reach across the country.

Building this philosophical framework is the job of the leader. This framework is built through consistent, effective communication and reinforcement of appropriate behavior. Once everyone understands the philosophical framework in which the company operates, delegation and empowerment can then—and only then—be effective.

One thing to remember: The communications effort must be ongoing. Silence often implies a change of direction. With new employees joining the company at the rate of, say, 10% a year, the philosophical framework message must be continually reinforced.

Even long-term employees often get the idea that *"this doesn't matter anymore because I haven't heard anything about it for a long time."*

You may get tired of carrying the message. But your people will not get tired of hearing it. Instead, it provides necessary reinforcement, letting your people know that what they're doing is consistent with the behavior the company deems important.

In my former company, every key person understood the framework in which the company operated. I had confidence that decisions being made by any of our key people would be consistent with that framework. We never had to pull the carpet out from under anybody.

But we worked continually at communicating the need to treat every constituency— employees, agents and policyholders—with total fairness and respect, with never an ethical lapse.

Many leaders tell me that they can spend their winter months in their condos in Florida or Hawaii and can be just as effective as they would be at their headquarters location in the cold north. *"I've got a telephone, a fax machine, and email,"* they say, *"so I can do everything that I would do if I were at the office."*

My answer to them is, *"Great! If you're my competitor, you're the kind of competitor I want."*

Communication is more than phone calls, emails and faxes. To delegate and empower effectively, you must be there and must continually reinforce the strategic direction of the company and the type of behavior that is expected.

Building a positive philosophical framework is one of a leader's most important activities and one that has a far-reaching impact on your company's success or failure.

5

GIVE ME THE MONEY

One of the jobs of a leader is to motivate people. That sounds simple enough. I've asked hundreds of people to whom I have spoken throughout the United States, "*What motivates you?*" I get the same answer perhaps 70% of the time.

"*Give me the money and I'll be motivated,*" most say.

Certainly money plays a role in motivation. But money by itself does not motivate. If money alone is a motivator, professional athletes and movie stars who make millions of dollars a year would always be motivated. But they're not. They need motivation just like you and me. Some may need motivation even more than most of us.

There are hundreds of examples of unhappy and unmotivated individuals—from professional athletes to factory workers—who are making significantly more than prevailing wage levels. Money alone simply doesn't get the job done.

As a matter of fact, money can become a demotivator. Some of the most demotivated people I know are in overpaid jobs. Over the past several years, I have talked to dozens of persons in senior management positions drawing huge salaries who tell me that they simply *"can't take it"* for another month. They're willing to accept another job, even with an appreciably smaller salary.

The reason that money can become a demotivator is that it tends to lock people into boring, unchallenging, dead-end jobs. They're making so much money they can't afford to move to jobs that provide greater stimulation and challenge.

The human being is meant to be challenged—to learn new things— to be "stretched."

Undoubtedly you've heard that people don't like change. Frankly, I don't buy it. I've tried this experiment with hundreds of groups throughout the country, and the result has always been the same.

I ask persons in the audience to raise their hands if they have at least 20 years remaining in their careers before they can retire at age 65. Then my offer goes like this:

"I'll give you a written contract to pay you $500,000 a year if you will perform your existing job in exactly the same manner—not a single detail will change—until you retire at age 65. You will get up at the same time, drive to the same office, sit at the same desk in the same chair, and perform the same duties, under the oversight of the same boss. How many of you will take me up on this offer?"

I normally get a sprinkling of hands.

A part of the proposition is that they are told that they must stick it out until retirement, not for just a year or two and quit. And performance must be acceptable. If they leave for any reason, the money must be returned with interest.

Then I extend the stakes—to $750,000 a year. Then $1 million a year.

Fewer than 10% of the group will respond positively, although this is far from a scientific survey.

"For those of you who did not raise your hands, how many of you believe they can do it?" I ask. There's always a resounding *"Nooooo."*

And I agree. It is virtually impossible to perform exactly the same job in exactly the same way for many years and remain excited and stimulated.

People must have new challenges in their lives. They must learn new things. If there are no changes and stimulation in their jobs, they go into the *"glide slope."* The performance glide slope normally rises for five years or so as a person is learning a new job. Then it levels out, but performance remains acceptable for a number of years even though there is no longer the stimulation of learning new things.

Then performance starts downhill ever so slowly. After 25 years or so of doing the same thing, we begin wondering why "ol' Joe or ol' Jane" had ever been hired. Actually, Joe and Jane were good performers 25 years ago. They have just become unmotivated and unchallenged for having to do the same ol' thing for 25 years or so. Performance starts to slip just a tad each year—until over a period of time performance dips to an unacceptable level.

I've found that if people are to be motivated and energized throughout their careers, they need new challenges in their job assignments every five to seven years.

The results of this experiment, and my own experience in my former company, have convinced me that people like change. If people don't want to do the same thing until they retire—and if they don't like change— what else is there?

What they don't like is having change crammed down their throats. They like to have some input into the matter. They need to be told the reason for the change and how it will be implemented. Lay all the facts on the table. And take your time in making the change. Normally a new procedure or activity need not be implemented over night.

Obviously employees don't like being caught off guard. They need to be sold.

It's normal to imagine the worst and to have concerns about accepting any new assignment. Deep down they're asking, "Am I smart enough to do this new job? Will I like my new boss? What happens to me if this new fangled idea doesn't work out? Will a geographic move be required?" The range of questions goes on and on.

Your people need assurance—even the top performers. They need to know that they are needed in your organization and have security and a future with your company. It is a part of your job as a leader to get the message across.

When offered different job assignments, I've been turned down dozens of times. *"I like what I'm doing now,"* they say.

"I'm glad you like your present job," I respond, *"but we really need a high-quality person in this job and we think you can do it.*

"May I suggest you try it for three months. If at the end of that three month period you don't like your new job, come back to me and we will either give you your old job or will find another job that you will like. You have done a great job here for many years and have contributed a great deal to this company. We

want you to remain a happy and productive employee. We'll make certain that you end up with a job you like."

Of the dozens of conversations I've had like this, not once has anyone said to me, *"I want to go back."* In every case I could see new energy and a revitalized spirit in the individuals with the new job assignments.

Nine months or so after one employee had been encouraged to take a new assignment for a three-month trial period, I ran into that employee's spouse. She came up and gave me a bear hug and said, *"Thank you so much for encouraging Mike to take that new job. He's so much happier. I'm so much happier. Even the kids are happier. Thank you, thank you, thank you."*

And remember, this was a job the employee thought he didn't want.

A friend of mine who recently retired as the CEO of a competing company was always in the process of reorganizing his company. I often chided him that he centralized his company during the even years and decentralized during the odd years. Obviously my accusation was an exaggeration, but I learned something about the management process by watching

38

his company from a distance. His company was in constant turmoil. People were being moved around often—from city to city—as one office closed and another absorbed the work. Certainly the constant reshuffling provided an opportunity for him to stimulate his people and get the right people in the right slot. People were challenged frequently. Ineffective people were not offered jobs after the reorganization. No one had an opportunity to become overly comfortable in any one job.

Perhaps his method worked. But I think it produced unnecessary stress and shock for the employees and their families. And the cost to relocate these folks was enormous.

I prefer to hire good people who have the ability to move upward in an organization and who are willing and able to accept new job challenges through the years.

Many employers say that employees are no longer loyal. The reason there is too little employee loyalty is because there is too little loyalty of the employer to the employee. If employers show loyalty to employees, most employees will reflect that loyalty.

How is it possible to offer new duties to employees every five to seven years? First, there tends to be a certain amount of change in every job. For instance, automation plays an increasingly important role in many, if not most, jobs in America, and with it comes greater stimulation and challenge.

Second, I'm a proponent of job posting. When a job opening occurs, post the job for all existing employees to see. List a summary of duties, skills required, and even the salary range. Any existing employee can apply, go through appropriate testing, interviews, etc., just like any outsider.

I'm an advocate of promoting insiders whenever possible. Too often insiders are excluded from consideration for promotion because we know their weaknesses. We also know their strengths and whether they have the ability to learn and grow. With outsiders we only know their strengths. Weaknesses are never advertised.

U.S. Department of Labor statistics show that workers between the ages of 18 and 40 go through 10.5 jobs over that 22 year period. With proper leadership techniques, that figure can be cut dramatically. Still a 10% turnover rate is relatively normal in most companies, even those with outstanding leadership—new mothers who decide to stay at home; employees who follow spouses who have been transferred; retirements; marginal or ineffective employees who have been requested to leave. (Fired employees should be less than one percent, however. If it's higher than that, it's a near sure sign that the selection process wasn't thorough enough. More on this later). With 10% turnover, in effect every job in the company turns over every 7.2 years. This means that there are opportunities to grow into more challenging job assignments in most companies.

Earlier in this chapter I said that money played a role in motivation. The role is this: Salary levels and benefits should be fair and competitive. I believe that every employee should receive the prevailing wage for comparable jobs in your industry and your community.

Each salary range should be adjusted annually for inflation, and the range should be wide enough that outstanding performance can be recognized.

Then exceptional employees can be further recognized as they move from Job A, to Job B, to Job C, etc.—jobs with progressively higher salary midpoints.

Salary incentive programs may also be appropriate, another topic we will discuss later.

Oh yes. If the word "change" bothers you, don't use that term. Call it *"improvement."* After all, if the change isn't an improvement, you shouldn't be making it.

Everyone likes improvement. And everyone loves opportunities that improvement brings about.

6

MAKING RECOGNITION WORK

Properly recognizing your people for a job well done is a critical dimension of great leadership.   But like money, recognition sometimes produces the opposite of the intended effect.

This principle came to my attention several years ago when I was eating breakfast in a Perkins Restaurant. While waiting to pay my check, I noticed a plaque on the wall headed **"Employee of the Month."** On it was inscribed the name of an outstanding employee for each month.   Beside it was another plaque for the prior year with the 12 names of the Employee of the Month.

My initial reaction was positive. *"Isn't it great that they're recognizing their good people,"* I said to myself.

As I paid my check, something bothered me about those plaques, so I reviewed them again. "This is a sham," I thought, for no name had been repeated for any month this year or the 12 months last year.

It's a near certainty that, if fairly administered, the Employee of the Month this month was the Employee of the Month last month, and will be the Employee of the Month next month. Great employees tend to be great employees—now and forever—unless we as leaders do something to mess up their performance.

Then I began to understand the forces at work. An Employee of the Month, especially one who receives the recognition consistently, will take heat from co-workers. *"Judy or Bill, what are you trying to prove? They don't appreciate what you're doing here. You're not going to make any more money than the rest of us. You're not going to get promoted any sooner than anyone else. All you're doing is showing up the rest of us. You're just a troublemaker."*

The employee's reaction is predictable. If you received the Employee of the Month designation on a regular basis, what would you do?

- - - - - **THE NEW LEADER** - - - - -

It's an unusual person who can take the harassment from associates and remain a top performer. Chances are your best employee will either slow down like all the others, or will quit. If he or she slows down or quits, the recognition program has produced just opposite of what you were trying to achieve—high performance.

The most positive thing that can happen is for Sharon, the consistent Employee of the Month, to ask management, *"Please don't designate me as the Employee of the Month again. I really like it here. This is the best job I've ever had. But I can't take the pressure from my cohorts."*

So management starts to pass around the designation, and employees soon recognize that the honor is not legitimate.

The most effective recognition programs make it possible for everyone, not just certain people, to make it over the bar if certain performance levels are achieved. In larger organizations, break the company down into branch offices, or geographic areas, or product lines—any logical division that has reasonably full control over profit and growth. When profit and growth targets are exceeded, everyone in that division should be recognized.

The more frequent the recognition, the better. Quarterly is better than annual. Monthly is better than quarterly. The high performance that is being recognized is too often forgotten, or employees believe it is unappreciated, if recognition is given too far in the future.

One of the best recognition programs, I have found, is some form of incentive compensation. It has the greatest value when paid monthly or quarterly (consistent with the employees' need for fast feedback). In a larger company, it is better to vary it by branch office, geographic area, product line or some easily defined profit center. Our purpose is to tie together the bonus, the company's success, and the performance of people so that everyone understands that this is a single mission.

To make such a bonus arrangement effective, there must be complete transparency in the company. All the numbers must be readily available to everyone. The formula must be easy to understand. And it must be based on definable, measurable, objective criteria, not subjective criteria that might be manipulated or subject to the opinion of managers. These requirements make it clear that such a bonus system is not for every company.

If employees feel that they are being flimflammed, the bonus system will not bring about the motivation and good will that you are hoping to achieve. It's imperative that employees be able to connect the bonus to performance. They have to understand that what they do produces the bonus. There must be a direct connect. This requires continuing communication from their leader. Otherwise the bonus becomes an entitlement and will not have a motivating effect.

Here's a general approach of how a bonus program might be structured. Begin with the total expenses of the company—a total of payroll, rent, taxes, electricity, gas, cost of goods sold, etc. In other words, what does it cost to open your door every morning, including non-cash items like depreciation.

If yours is a for-profit company, add to the other overhead costs a small but reasonable return to the owners for the use of their money—let's say 8% or 10% of their investment.

Share a portion of the profit above these costs with all employees as a percentage of base salary. Ten percent of the profit pool might be an appropriate target to consider. In a larger organization, allocate that amount by the contribution of each profit center. Employees in the corporate arena and not affiliated with just one profit center should receive an average of all profit centers.

There should be a companywide "trigger"— that is, the company must be profitable overall before the bonus is payable. But once the trigger is activated, the bonus is paid based on each profit center's contribution to the company's bottom line.

Such a plan won't work in all companies because financial information is not available to everyone. Yet, when financial information is shared, I believe strongly that an incentive compensation plan of this type will produce a team of people committed to making the company a success and will run circles around the secretive company that has not achieved worker buy-in.

The way to get that commitment is to bring employees into the circle. Make them feel like owners. Show them that their contributions are related directly to the company's success or failure. Give them access to the financials. Don't hide anything from them. If it's a public corporation they can get the financials anyway. The 10K's and 10Q's are available on the Internet. Very few things in the company need to be kept secret.

How can your company remain competitive when it pays a bonus and many competitors don't? I pointed out earlier that you may be wasting as much as 70% of your payroll on disengaged employees—people who are not committed to making your company a success. If you can create a highly energized, committed, gung-ho workforce, you have that margin to work with. The upside potential is huge.

I'm not suggesting that you increase base salaries above those paid by your competitors. The base should be prevailing wage levels in your industry and your community. If you are to be competitive with other companies, that's all you can afford to pay and stay in business. The bonuses come from high-level performance that your competitors are not getting.

Auto manufacturer BMW has a pay for performance plan that dates back to 1972, and they have unparalleled worker harmony in the auto business. It distributes as much as one and a half months' extra pay to workers at the end of the year—or about 12½% of a worker's annual salary. The union has permitted schedule flexibility to meet production demands, and no one can remember layoffs at BMW.

I toured the BMW plant in Spartanburg, South Carolina, and learned that the assembly line is formed like a small letter e. The assembly process starts at the tail end of the e, travels around the circle, and the beautiful new BMW rolls off the assembly line at the hash mark in the middle of the e. The reason for this, I was told, was to permit everyone along the line to see the beautiful new car to which the worker was contributing. This relates to the fast feedback point I made earlier—very unusual in a manufacturing environment.

BMW understands the value of both fast feedback and pay for performance. In the Munich plant, unfinished car bodies and assembly components travel on a track above offices and the cafeteria. Everyone in the plant can feel the pulse of the plant change when there's a problem. There's an atmosphere of togetherness and openness.

- - - - - THE NEW LEADER - - - - -

The human resources department at the BMW plant in Germany receives more than 200,000 applications annually. Those who make the first cut undergo a day-long interview process. Everybody wants to work there. Compare this environment to the domestic auto manufacturers that are struggling to stay alive.

If some form of incentive compensation plan is not possible, at least buy lunch every month for every employee when the company or department meets its profit objective. Or order in pizza. Do something to let them know that their contributions are appreciated.

Other forms of recognition are also appropriate. In my former company, we quoted in the company newsletter favorable comments from customers about the performance of any one of our people. President's Circle pins (a small company logo with a circle around it)—gold, silver, and bronze versions for first, second and third year winners—were given to those who achieved certain sales levels. We had SweepSteaks (yes, Steaks) for branch offices that achieved their goals. I went to the branch, donned a chef's hat and apron, fired up gas grills, and prepared steaks for every employee.

Be innovative. Many forms of recognition are appropriate—as long as the recognition is legitimate. If employees are rewarded for showing up for work, the recognition will have little effect on overall performance and soon becomes an entitlement.

All forms of recognition require that the company operate in an atmosphere of total communications, upward and downward; trust; friendliness; great relationships between management and employees. Associates will not be motivated in a hostile, threatening, intimidating work environment. The age of the imperial boss is over. Yet this is still the norm in many American businesses.

Building an open, friendly, non-threatening, communicative organization starts with a smile. Smile when you see your employees. It doesn't hurt, I promise. When I visit corporations, time after time I've walked down the hallway with the CEO. I smiled and spoke to everybody I saw, people I had never seen before and probably will never see again, while the CEO with me walked through these folks as if they weren't there.

There cannot be communication without trust—and it's unusual to have trust without a smile.

52

So smile—and call them by their first name—
and encourage them to call you by your first
name.

A highly capable high school teacher said that
one of her best principals had asked that he
be addressed by his first name. *"He had my
full respect, and I felt that communication was
easier,"* she said.

I visited one company where it was company
policy not to speak to anyone on a lower
level than you were. That company had been
experiencing difficult times and recently sold.
It is no surprise.

Someone asked, *"How do you maintain the
respect of your subordinates when you permit
them to call you by your first name?"*

*"If an employee calls you Joe or Mr. Brown,
does respect really change? If they don't
respect us, they're going to call us a lot of
things worse than our first names when we're
not around,"* I answered.

The first objection usually cited to calling
employees by name is, *"I'm not good with
names."* Well, nobody is until they develop
the skill. Learn one new name a day. It won't

take long until you know practically everyone's first name, even in a sizable organization.

Keep a four by six inch card with the name of your direct reports, maybe the next level as well. In a smaller organization, list all employees. Now jot down the name of the employee's spouse, the names of the kids, their ages, where they go to school, their hobbies, the name of the dog, everything. There are computer programs to keep this type of information, but I find a card is easier to use and just as helpful.

When you know you're going to be visiting with a certain employee, glance at the information before the visit.

"Great idea," one manager told me, *"I'll send out a questionnaire."* No, don't send out a questionnaire. Jot down the information when it comes out in casual conversations.

Employees will care about you and your company when you show that you care about them and their families.

Your employees back at their work stations right now have every problem conceivable to mankind. They have financial problems, marital problems, kid problems, career problems, health problems. You name them, they've got them. Some of them handle the problems pretty well; others do not.

They need someone to talk to now and then. They need to feel free to share problems with you; maybe they'll want your advice; they may need someone to help them think through a personal difficulty.

An employee's first concern is his or her family and personal welfare. Therefore, your concern for your employees must be a high priority. When your employees legitimately believe that you care about them, they will care about you. When you care about them, and they know your concern is sincere, they will give their full allegiance and commitment to you and your company.

I am often asked, *"How can we create an environment of trust, friendliness, compassion and kindness, creating that favorable employee-employer relationship, when employee layoffs are required?"* Certainly layoffs are sometimes necessary. If you can't meet Friday's payroll, obviously dire action must be taken.

But generally I believe that layoffs are not necessary. In nearly every case, layoffs make the company weaker, not stronger.

Let's say your company has announced that 20% of its employees must go. Every employee thinks that he or she might be affected. So each one goes home that night and polishes up the old resume.

Should a headhunter or a competitor call with an opportunity to explore a job, and they often do when there's a layoff announcement, every single employee will check it out.

Which employees are most likely to be called by competitors or headhunters? The best employees—not mediocre ones or weaker ones.

The best employees leave with job knowledge, competitive information, and usually outstanding customer goodwill. The weaker employees remain because they didn't have an opportunity to move.

So the company becomes weaker—although it did meet its objective of reducing employee count by 20%.

If layoffs are absolutely necessary, get it behind you quickly. When the announcement is made, also announce the employees who will be affected and tell the remaining employees that they have a secure job for the long term. This will permit you to keep your most valuable people.

Again, generally layoffs are not necessary. Financial problems didn't occur over the past weekend. The problems have been creeping up for months, maybe even years. Don't wait to reduce staff. Do it early in the game, not late in the game, and handle the reduction through normal attrition.

With nearly every layoff announcement in the newspapers, less than 10% of the staff is involved. What is a normal attrition rate? For most well-managed businesses, usually about 10%. Handling staff reduction through normal attrition solves a host of morale and productivity issues.

Recognition that works involves building an organization in which your people are informed about all phases of the operation; an organization in which your people will buy into the mission; an organization in which your people will feel they are a part of a winning team; an organization in which your people will commit themselves to going the extra mile to serve customers and make your company the best in its industry.

Throughout this process you reward your people with appropriate forms of recognition, perhaps additional compensation, and great personal relationships.

7

SPAN OF NO CONTROL

The way many American companies are organized reminds me of an old childhood game we sometimes played on cold winter days in my one-room Kansas school. The first person whispered a short story to the next child in a circle. The second whispered it to the third, the third to the fourth, and so on. The last person in the circle repeated the story aloud. The group usually laughed because as the story was passed from one child to the next, it changed enough that it had become nonsensical. (Yes, without television or computer games, we were easy to entertain in those days).

Through the years the game has had a number of names, among them "Telephone" or "Gossip." This game serves as an example of a concept in modern-day American business known as span of control. This term represents the number of employees a leader can be responsible for and can communicate with effectively. In the Telephone or Gossip game, the span of control is one—one person reporting to one person. The greater the number of people getting the message through this narrow span of control, the more distorted the message becomes.

Too often I see companies with spans of control that are too narrow, some even with one-on-one reporting arrangements. When one person has one direct report, or even two or three direct reports, generally someone is unnecessary. Narrow spans of control create multiple layers of management and costly bureaucratic overhead that make communication, both upward and downward, nearly impossible. The span of control becomes a span of no control.

Giant corporations in America often have 15 to 20 layers of management. Mid-sized companies sometimes have 10 or 12. This is too many for effective communication. Additionally, this arrangement adds too much expense and makes decision making too slow.

Efficient, nimble competitors will run circles around the stodgy organization burdened by too many layers of management.

It is better to have a span of control that is too wide than to have too many layers of management. Those of us in management positions may not like to hear this, but management is an overhead expense. Too many companies spend an inordinate amount of payroll expense at the top of the management pyramid and are too quick to cut payroll at the bottom of the pyramid—the people on the firing line who are serving customers.

In my former company our policy was never to have more than five layers, and in many departments there were fewer. Even very large companies—significantly larger than ours—can operate with no more than five layers. Let's do the math. If the span of control is capped at ten, a five-layer system can accommodate more than 11,000 employees.

It may be advisable to have fewer direct reports at the top of the management pyramid and more direct reports at the bottom of the pyramid, but in any event five layers should be a maximum for most organizations.

In smaller organizations, with 10 to 50 employees, two or three layers are more appropriate.

Every management layer adds another communication hurdle. As in the childhood game, information is screened and distorted a number of times. Ultimately, the boss gets inaccurate information or only knows what those at the lower levels want the boss to know.

Great ideas that would cut expense or improve service—from those best able to generate ideas, the people actually doing the work— never make it through the system. Someone someplace in the management structure lets it die. This inaction dries up the source of other great ideas. Good employees will say, *"You didn't take action on my last idea. Why should I submit others?"*

If a good idea actually survives the multiple layers, it isn't unusual for others to take credit. Surveys have shown that 70% of employees say their managers have taken credit for their ideas. In the future, these folks will probably be unwilling to make other suggestions that would benefit the organization.

Multiple management layers slow down the decision-making process.

And when the decision is made, it may be made based on incomplete information because all the facts surrounding the matter didn't make it through the management maze.

The successful company of the future must be nimble, adjusting quickly to economic and competitive developments.

Then there's the issue of cost. I've seen companies that have allocated two-thirds of their payroll to management-level employees and only one-third to those who are actually serving customers. There is something wrong with this picture.

Too often we see co-supervisors, co-managers, and even co-CEOs. The most successful co-anything I've ever found is marriage, and it works only about 50% of the time. In a business environment, co-whatever will work less often.

While this arrangement is healthy in a home environment, it's still a struggle at times. Kids ask mom if they can go to a movie. She says "*no*," so they ask dad. Before long they know whom to ask for what. They learn that dad is more likely to let them go to the movies with the other kids; mom is more likely to let the youngster borrow the car to visit a friend. The kids work one parent against the other.

So it goes at work. Employees will learn which co-manager will more likely react favorably to certain issues. Communication, upward and downward, becomes even worse as both co-managers are kept somewhat in the dark. I've found that co-managers are just as unhappy with this arrangement as the people who report to them.

Why are co-managers appointed? Perhaps there are valid reasons I have been unable to unearth, but the co-managers I've observed were selected because their superiors had two good people they didn't want to disappoint. When both were chosen, both were disappointed.

You can be more effective as a leader in a lean, relatively flat organization. Upward and downward communication is improved; your company can be more responsive to changing conditions; and efficiency is enhanced. Furthermore, employees are happier and more likely to commit themselves to the company's success when bureaucracy is held to a minimum.

8

'HOW AM I DOING?'

Your people want to know, and need to know, how they're doing. Therefore, every person needs a written performance evaluation at least once a year. But an annual written evaluation by itself is not adequate.

The written evaluation should be supplemented with many "pats on the back" whenever deserved throughout the year.

And when there's a weakness in performance, coaching is in order. Every employee deserves to know when some aspect of his or her performance is not up to par, and each individual should be given an opportunity to improve. It's a small investment to coach each employee to higher levels of achievement.

Coaching need not have an adversarial tone. It may be as simple as asking the employee, "*If you were doing this again tomorrow, would you handle it differently?"* A discussion of alternatives for handling a situation has great value in helping an employee become stronger and more competent in every dimension of the job.

Time after time I've found that written evaluations fail to provide the positive feedback that the employee needs or to recommend appropriate corrective action.

Situations like this are not uncommon: *"I think we're going to have to fire Joe,"* a supervisor reports to you. *"His performance continues to deteriorate, despite my continual coaching and insistence he must show improvement."*

The supervisor makes a good case that Joe must go. Then you decide to review Joe's written performance evaluations over the past two or three years to see if the problems with his performance had been properly documented and to be certain that specific steps to overcome his performance deficiencies had been recommended to Joe.

According to his evaluations, Joe performed most aspects of his job very well, even above average, and improvement was suggested in only a few minor areas. And the suggestions for improvement were not stated in such a way that Joe had reason to believe that his career was in jeopardy. Furthermore, his salary increases each year were in line with company averages.

It's as if two persons were being evaluated. (1) Joe's performance evaluations are relatively favorable—maybe a few deficiencies, but nothing significant. Salary increases are in line with company averages. (2) *"I can't put up with Joe's shoddy performance any longer,"* his supervisor now insists. "We have no choice but to fire him."

When an employee is recommended for termination because of poor performance, I've found that many performance appraisals do nothing to support the termination. Managers and supervisors have emphasized the employee's positive personal and work characteristics and have played down, even glossed over, the negatives.

I'm convinced it's all Mom's fault. Mom taught us since early childhood, *"If you can't say something nice about someone, don't say it."* The lesson took—even when evaluating employees.

Not only are the written evaluations often deceptive, but oral comments to the worker are often likewise misleading. On several occasions through the years I've talked to employees who were being terminated, and I believed them when they told me that they did not know that their performance was unacceptable.

There's nothing wrong with saying nice things about good performers. In fact, it's an absolute necessity if we are to keep our people motivated. For many people the annual performance evaluation is the only expression of appreciation they receive throughout the year.

To keep morale high—and to get the very best from your people—that annual *"pat on the back"* must be complemented by many other forms of appreciation. In your daily association with employees, compliment good performance whenever you see it. Pass on to them the compliments about them you may have received from customers. When someone goes beyond the call of duty to give outstanding customer service, thank him or her and express your appreciation.

The more compliments you give to your people about excellent customer service, the more instances of excellent customer service you'll have to compliment. People respond positively to praise.

All forms of praise must be genuine, however. If you inadvertently compliment a person in a department who is not a top performer, or perhaps even on probation, everyone in the department will know that your comments are insincere. Your credibility will be lost.

A principal role of leadership is to motivate people—and one of the great motivators is a genuine *"thank you"* or *"we appreciate you."*

A leader also has an obligation to do everything possible to help improve the skills of people through continual coaching, training, motivation and encouragement. Helping people develop their full potential is not only the right thing to do, it makes sense economically. It often costs a lot to terminate an employee, and it costs a lot to hire and train another employee. After the dust settles, there's always a chance—a good chance—that the new employee will possess even fewer performance skills than the one just terminated.

There are, of course, times when termination is in order. When an employee is involved in dishonest acts, I recommend a zero tolerance policy. No second chance.

When performance problems persist, I suggest the "three strikes and you're out" approach.

Step 1 – Identify specifically in writing the nature of the performance problems and outline specifically what the employee must do to perform at an acceptable level—*"or we must take more serious action."* At this point, don't define what you mean by "more serious action."

Step 2 – Review the individual's performance in writing three months later. If progress has been made in specific areas, make specific note of these improvements. If progress has not been made, reiterate the nature of the performance problems specifically in writing and again outline specifically what must be done for the employee to do acceptable work. Close the evaluation with these words: *"If sufficient progress isn't made in another three months, we will have no choice but to terminate your service with our company."*

Step 3 – Either performance will have improved, or you will terminate. No waffling. The employee has been adequately warned.

Termination is never easy. The night before I would fire someone, I probably got a lot less sleep than the person I was firing.

"*You are not happy here,*" I've often said to a person who is being terminated. In every case—I can't think of an exception—the answer has been, "*No, I'm not happy here.*"

"*You'll never be successful unless you find something you love,*" I continue. "*Nobody has ever been successful working a job they don't like. Truly successful people always love what they do. We sincerely hope that you too will find a new career that you love and in which you will be successful. Good luck to you, and may God bless you.*"

We shake hands and the termination is complete. It wasn't easy—but it wasn't a combative slugfest either. Mom would want you to handle a termination like this.

And despite what Mom might have said when you were a child, she would want you to give honest and helpful feedback—both positive and negative—whenever it can help a person become more successful.

That's your job as a leader.

9

BUILDING NEW
TEAM MEMBERS

Many American businesses cite employee turnover as one of their biggest management problems. *"We just can't get good people,"* managers say, *"and when we get them, we can't keep them."* A shocking statistic is that half of new hires quit or are fired within six months.

The U. S. Department of Labor tells us that workers between the ages of 18 and 40 go through 10.5 jobs over that 22 year period. That's a job move nearly every two years.

By applying the principles outlined in this book, you should be able to keep most of your good people. Still, with a normal attrition rate of say 10%, in effect you face the problem of having to replace every employee every 7.2

years. Therefore, it's imperative that new team members be selected with caution.

Too often employees are chosen under less than ideal conditions. Studies have shown that relying on the average interview to fill a job opening is only 7% more accurate than flipping a coin.

I've found that managers in most companies are too quick to hire and too slow to fire. Therefore, it makes sense to spend more time hiring so you can spend less time firing.

Recruiting is a costly process. Additional expense is involved for advertising, interviewing, as well as the paperwork required to bring new employees on board. Training is expensive and time consuming, even for capable new employees. More of your time is required to bring new people up to speed and to bring about understanding of the culture and the service orientation of your organization.

There tends to be an error ratio of 10% to 20%, even when the hiring process is handled in a thorough manner. An outstanding interviewer with a keen people-selection instinct still makes mistakes. It's a lot harder to get rid of people who will not perform or cannot perform than it was to hire them.

Furthermore, termination often brings about charges of discrimination because of age, sex, or some type of alleged disability that no one considered consequential at the time of hiring. This happens often enough that it's imperative that you exercise extraordinary caution when hiring new people.

Interviews often are sketchy. Too often interviewers do more talking than the interviewee. At the conclusion of a half-hour interview, it sometimes turns out that the manager is the one who has been interviewed while learning very little about the candidate for employment.

Even during well-structured interviews, there is only so much one can learn during a 30 or 60 minute session. Some candidates have learned how to beat the system by giving answers we want to hear. There are web sites and college classes that help people learn how to answer interview questions appropriately. Unfortunately, an interview that consists of fabricated answers will not necessarily tell us anything about how a person will perform on the job.

Resumes are often misleading. Of the hundreds of resumes I've reviewed through the years, I've never read a bad one. Most are perfect or nearly perfect, placing a positive light on almost every aspect of a person's experience and performance. Many are prepared by outsourcing firms or professional resume services, not by the job candidate.

"Save the envelopes in which resumes are enclosed," I once asked the HR department of my former company. It was my contention that the envelopes, often with illegible handwriting and misspelled words, tell us more about the potential employee than the resumes themselves.

But there's a way to improve your odds. A number of years ago at my former company, we were involved in a delicate situation involving an unproductive employee when I happened to read about a Japanese company that conducted a full day of interviews with each candidate for employment. The process had so greatly improved its success in hiring good people that I put such a plan into effect in our company. Following an interview and preliminary screening by the human resources department, each applicant was to be interviewed by no fewer than five individuals (who received special interview training), three of whom were not in the hiring department.

The process cut our hiring mistakes in half—from the 18% to 20% range to the 8% to 10% range. The hiring mistake factor was determined by a survey of managers: "How many people did you hire over the past 12 month period who are not as good as you would like?" The newly hired people may have been average performers, but they were not superior performers. The surveys told us we were still making some hiring mistakes, but we had cut that mistake factor in half.

There were several reasons for the improvement. The involvement of several interviewers caused the hiring department to take the hiring process more seriously. And when the interviewers were all from the hiring department, the questions asked tended to be more technical in nature, specific to the particular job being filled. Interviewers from the non-hiring department were more likely to focus on other attributes of the candidate: attitude, team spirit, value system, work ethic, ability and willingness to learn, and the like.

Following the cross interviews, the hiring department made the final decision, but the hiring manager had the benefit of several viewpoints that proved to be of great value.

What do prospective employees think about all the fuss of cross interviews? Without exception, they were impressed. They feel good about being associated with a company that spends so much time with a candidate for employment. They feel special when they are selected from a number of good candidates by several interviewers. And the process permits them to learn more about the company and become acquainted with several managers. With the cross interview process, everybody wins.

Another hiring principle that will improve morale and the quality of new employees is to adopt a nepotism policy. That is, relatives should not work within the jurisdiction of the parent (or grandparent, uncle, aunt, or what have you). This is not to say that kids of the CEO or other managers are not good employees. They may be the best in the world; nevertheless, other employees tend to feel, first, they are spies and will communicate every indiscretion to the boss, creating tension throughout the organization. Secondly, coworkers imagine that *"they make more money than I do;"* or *"they get away with more than I possibly can. If I did that, I'd get fired."*

I think it's safe to say that sons and daughters of the big boss do tend to get favorable treatment. I know this to be true. At several points in my career, relatives of the big boss reported to me, and I can tell you with certainty that it is difficult at times to take appropriate action.

And such an arrangement is not good for the young employee. He or she never knows for sure, *"Did I succeed? Or did Mom or Dad succeed for me?"*

My suggestion is that children (and close friends, I might add) develop their own careers elsewhere. Should they join the parent's company later, it's easier for them, and they're more readily accepted by associates, when they have achieved some degree of business success elsewhere.

The best predictor of the future performance of any individual is how that person has performed in the past. The difficulty, of course, is the information about that performance is nearly always sketchy—and sometimes exaggerated beyond reality— unless the employee is already on the payroll.

This is why I prefer to hire people for lower-level jobs who have the ability and the desire to grow into jobs with greater responsibilities. This gives employees the new challenges and stimulation they require every few years if they are to remain motivated workers.

Correcting, disciplining or eliminating marginal workers is a slow, demanding, and expensive process. That's why it's imperative to make the selection process as thorough as possible.

10

CHECKING WITH THE REAL EXPERTS

My wife and I eat out often. We stopped for breakfast at a new restaurant that made a good first impression—pleasant surroundings, good service, good food—but the coffee must have been the worst in the state.

Being forgiving people and knowing that everyone has a bad day now and then, we decided that the coffee on that particular day must have been an exception and we tried the restaurant again several days later. Again, the service and food were good, but the coffee was horrible.

Not wanting to be labeled a complainer, I asked our server in my kindest voice if she ever had complaints about the coffee. *"Oh yes, all the time,"* she answered, *"but there's nothing I can do about it. It's a management decision."*

"Does your manager know that people often complain about the coffee?" I continued.

"Yes, I've mentioned it to her, but she can't do anything about it either. You see, it's a management decision."

A few minutes later the manager appeared at our table. *"I'm told you don't like the coffee,"* she said. *"We do get complaints about it, but there's nothing I can do about it. It's a management decision."* Then she explained that the "big boss" makes decisions for all his restaurants. He negotiates a good deal, and there's nothing she can do about it.

"Has it occurred to you or the boss," I continued, *"that you'd have many more customers if you had good coffee? It's likely that most people don't say anything about the coffee. They simply don't return. Your coffee is probably costing you a lot of money."*

Then she told me that if I didn't like the coffee, I should email the boss and maybe I could get something done about it.

Following this encounter, I started counting the number of times I've had similar responses from employees of various businesses. I ran out of fingers.

A few years ago we moved from our farm to the city. I called the cable television company to start cable service at our new home but was told, "We can't begin cable service for you. There is an unpaid bill at that address."

"Well, it's not my bill," I replied. *"Are you suggesting that I pay the bill of the previous owner?"*

"That's our policy," she answered, *"and there's nothing I can do about it. It's a management decision."*

I thanked her, and we continued the dish TV service we had at the farm. Of course, the cable company is still in business, but absent at least one paying customer.

Are similar circumstances occurring in your organization? Are customers being served properly? Are customers being driven to competitors? The only way to know for certain is to ask the real experts, those who work with customers on a day to day basis.

Most leaders spend an inordinate amount of management time with employees who do not follow instructions. Yet a leader's investment of time will pay greater dividends if more management time is spent with the majority of employees who do follow instructions.

Most people do exactly as they are told—to the nth degree—even when inappropriate, even when the rule they are conscientiously applying damages customer relationships, even when their actions may have a severe negative impact on the business.

Certainly some American workers are apathetic about their jobs and take little pride in their jobs and the companies for which they work. Also, technology, while having a positive impact on efficiency, has created an impersonal environment in the business world, making it more difficult for employees to communicate with customers.

For the most part, however, instances like those I've cited occur because employees feel they are being good soldiers and are simply doing what they're told.

Your employees know your customers and their problems and concerns better than anyone. They know when a process can be changed to make it more customer friendly. It's up to you as their leader to talk to employees on a regular basis to find out how customer service can be improved.

Ask them about complaints they've heard from customers. Ask them what customers like most about your products or services. Ask them what customers like least about your products or services. Ask them about improvements that can be made to please customers more. Are there rules that are driving customers away? Your people are the real experts. Ask them!

Until you ask them, many employees will be fearful about disagreeing with a standing rule or policy. They may think you don't want to know. They may believe that you think you have all the answers. And they may think they'll get fired if they tell you something that they believe you don't want to hear.

Early in my career I once suggested to my boss that we offer to our customers a certain product that had been introduced by one of our major competitors. I had estimated its cost and the value and it appeared to be a good investment. He replied, "*If you think Company X is so great, why don't you work there?*"

Thereafter, I seldom made a suggestion as long as I reported to this individual, nor did my associates when they heard about my experience. Reactions like this cause employees to be reluctant to make suggestions or pass on customer complaints. And that's why it may take awhile for two-way communication with your people to open up.

When you've identified a problem, take action—quickly. Action lets your people know that you really want to know how to serve customers better, that you will not interpret a suggestion as criticism of your company or the boss, and that the messenger will be appreciated and honored, not shot.

That's why I believe that every business, no matter how large or small, needs to hold regularly scheduled sales meetings. (Every employee of every business is involved in sales, whether or not the sales activity is shown in job descriptions). The meeting need last only five or ten minutes, ideally every week but no more infrequently than monthly. Have coffee and donuts and a good, open two-way conversation about serving customers better. These are great forums for creating an open-communication culture that is essential for successful businesses.

Although employees may be slow to respond initially, over time they will become more comfortable with making suggestions. And they will become more aware of customer needs and concerns, knowing they have a forum in which to share their suggestions.

The information provided by employees will be far better than can be gleaned from focus groups or customer surveys. By taking action on the information employees provide, you will notice that gradually customers will receive better service, your organization will become more successful, and your employee team will become more enthusiastic, vital contributors to a winning organization.

11

WHEN NOT TO COMMUNICATE

You know by now that great leaders must be great communicators. Most dimensions of leadership require thorough, ongoing communication.

But leaders also have the responsibility of knowing when not to communicate. Leaders must know how to keep confidential information confidential.

"I heard some folks talking about you at the airport the other day," a next-door neighbor told me.

"Was it complimentary?" I asked.

"Well......not really," he answered. *"It had something to do with computer software, and*

they gave me the impression that you are not their favorite person."

He gave me the date of his business trip. After checking my calendar, I knew the names of the people who were giving me a not-too-favorable public evaluation. I can't be too critical of them because at the time I wouldn't have named any of these software peddlers to the Salespersons' Hall of Fame.

Too many of us believe that the anonymity of those around us somehow provides a shroud of secrecy around our personal and business conversations.

"But there was a lot of noise and nobody was listening," it can be argued.

You're at a party with dozens or hundreds of people, all talking at once, creating a buzz that would drown out the engines of a 747. There's so much chatter that you feel confident that your conversation is relatively private. Then someone across the room mentions your name. Your ears perk up. Your name and bits of the conversation surrounding it stand out from the hubbub. We've all had this experience.

I've been on airplanes, trying to concentrate on reading materials or working on a business project, when the word "insurance" or the name of a competitor cuts through the noise. My attention shifts from my task to the conversation taking place nearby. On one occasion two officials of a competing insurance company were on the way to a state insurance department to file a rate change. I didn't pick up helpful competitive information, but you can bet I listened intently.

On another occasion, two employees of a company were doing a near-public evaluation of another employee. *"It looks like we're going to have to let Sarah go. We've tried and tried to get her up to speed and she just hasn't responded. We have no other option."*

I didn't know the two people involved in the discussion, and I didn't know Sarah. But somebody on the plane might have picked up just enough of the conversation to identify Sarah, who is perhaps a relative, a friend or a neighbor.

Cell phone use is especially abused. According to one source, there are some 193 million cell phones in the United States alone, and it sometimes seems that all 193 million callers believe that nobody can hear their conversation except the person on the other end of the call.

I've heard conversations on pricing of certain products—products I can't identify, but perhaps a competitor sitting just feet away can use that information to advantage.

I've heard conversations about hiring an especially valuable person from another company. Again, I didn't know the people or the company, but someone nearby might have been able to put together bits of the conversation and identify the employee and/or the company.

Public use of cell phones often amounts to legal wiretaps. *The world is listening.* And what the world hears can be injurious.

Even if it's not damaging, it's rude. Forcing those nearby to listen to personal or business conversations can be as intrusive as a noisy neighbor playing a boom box at full blast on a Sunday afternoon.

Perhaps we can forgive the person who inadvertently leaves a cell phone on during church or a business meeting; however, to answer the phone in such circumstances is never acceptable.

- - - - - **Robert L. Bailey** - - - - -

Here are a few simple rules about when not to communicate:

• Any non-public information should be discussed only in the privacy of an office or conference room, never by cell phone or in public. Competitors are always looking for any information that may give them an advantage.

• Discussion of personnel matters likewise should be held in private. Discussions that reach the wrong people can be embarrassing and even slanderous.

• Leaders and people in your organization are expected to conduct themselves in a friendly, courteous, gentlemanly or lady-like manner—always. A customer or prospective customers may relate an intrusive cell phone call, objectionable language, or rude behavior to your company, whose name might be identified through one end of the phone conversation or by a company logo on a luggage tag. "That's not the kind of people I want to deal with," an important customer might say.

Those of us who were in business in pre-cell phone days may have an advantage. We learned that it isn't necessary to be in touch with the world 24/7. None of us is that important. Chances are that people back at the office can take care of most matters just as well as we can, if not better.

Turn off the cell phone. Check voice mail periodically. Return important calls when it's not an imposition on people nearby and when confidential matters cannot be overheard.

Cell phones can be a form of eavesdropping and can have serious ramifications on a business. Their use should not be taken lightly.

12

THE FUTURE

"The future ain't what it used to be," said the famous baseball player and manager Yogi Berra.

Despite Yogi's profound insight, it's possible to predict the future with reasonably great precision, and the process doesn't require mind readers, psychics, palm readers or clairvoyants. Predicting the future falls within your job description as a leader.

Successful leaders tend to be excellent planners, and excellent planning requires a good track record of predicting the future.

How do effective leaders go about predicting the future? They observe and study the trends that have occurred in their particular industry over the years. History repeats itself in many ways.

They observe the developments in other industries. And they see the relationship of trends in other industries with advances in their own industry.

If you're a voracious reader (and I encourage you to be one), trends are easier to identify. Two or three articles about a new development or customer demand in auto sales, women's clothing, fast food, television, or any other industry may reveal a trend or consumer demand that is developing in your own field.

A look at history and the world around us reveals a great deal about the future.

Based on your own experience in your field— and your observations of other businesses throughout your lifetime—consider these questions.

In ten years:

• Will there be more or fewer companies in your type of business in the United States?

• Will there be a greater squeeze on profits, or will profits be easier to achieve?

- Will there be greater pressure to reduce expenses or will expense levels be less important?

- Will consumers require faster service, or will they be happy with more relaxed levels of service?

- Will automation play a greater or smaller role in your business?

- Will government be more intrusive or less intrusive in your business life?

- Will government be more intrusive or less intrusive in your personal life?

- Will there be a more global economy or more of a trend toward an isolationist U.S. economy that may affect your business?

There's little doubt but that you answered these questions correctly. It's possible to assemble a hundred questions like these, appropriate for your own industry, and you can answer the questions accurately because the trend has been firmly established as far back as any of us can remember.

Many things that happen in our businesses are nothing more than a continuation of trends that have been developing over the course of a lifetime. There are few surprises. Perhaps the speed of change has accelerated, but the established trends continue.

We know there will continue to be consolidation in most industries in America because history makes the trend clear.

We know there will be a greater squeeze on profits and expenses because that's been true for many years, regardless of industry. It's more difficult to make a living today in most fields of business.

We know that consumers will require not just fast service but almost instant service. The trend is clear. It's a fast food, fast everything culture. Consumers want service when it's convenient for them, not necessarily when it's convenient for you.

Consumers want more options, not fewer options. It's becoming increasingly obvious that one size doesn't fit all. The fast food combo allows the buyer to substitute a baked potato or salad for the fries, or kids can substitute applesauce for fries and milk for the soft drink.

- - - - - Robert L. Bailey - - - - -

There is a dizzying array of new cars on the market, a dramatic contrast to the days when you could buy a Model T Ford in any color you wanted as long as it was black. Today new auto buyers can select from some 260 models. There are 31 types of Pop-Tarts and 90 types of pantyhose from which buyers can choose.

Not only do restaurants have wine lists, they also have bottled water lists.

As options increase, buyers must be better informed. And the need for better informed buyers requires better informed salespeople. And as options increase, processing complexities increase.

There's little doubt that technology will play an increasingly significant role in virtually all industries. No matter how slick the technology, no matter how state-of-the-art it is, no matter how large the investment in technology, we can be reasonably certain that somebody, someplace, has just invented something that makes current technology obsolete.

Still, there are trends in technology that can be accurately predicted. For instance, it's likely that the capabilities of your current equipment and software are being utilized only marginally. You can do a lot more with what you have. If your equipment and software vendors are still providing service, a huge additional investment in technology may not be required at this time. You need not be on the *"bleeding edge."* It's often better to be a fast follower. Learn from the mistakes of your competitors.

When analyzing technology, don't think in terms of hardware and software. Think in terms of processes. Eliminate slow, costly and cumbersome assembly lines. Leading-edge companies capture all information at the source and make it available instantly to anyone who needs it in the form it is needed. This is the way to reduce overhead costs and provide the instant service that consumers demand.

In my former industry, it was once common to pass a new business transaction from the underwriting department, to the rating department, to the coding department, to data entry, to the file department, etc. Throughout the process, the policy information was not available to anyone else.

Now it's a one-stop process, with most transactions being submitted by local agents located in the customers' neighborhoods across the country. Information is available to everyone immediately. If a claim occurs even on the day of submission, the claim department can take appropriate action immediately.

As you're planning to grow and prosper for the long term, keep in mind that one thing has not changed, yet it's overlooked more often than any other dimension in long-range planning. ***People like to do business with people.***

Customers want to be treated like guests in your home. They want every business transaction to be a pleasant experience— no hassles—painless. The American people are screaming for friendly, caring, personal service. Pleasant, friendly, hassle-free service will offset most of the technology problems that tend to strangle so many organizations.

As a leader, there's a lot on your plate. You must keep your operation running efficiently and profitably today by building a team of dedicated people committed to making your business a success. And you must also look to the future so that appropriate adjustments can be made in your operations to assure your organization's success for the long term.

13

THEY'RE MAKING ADULTS YOUNGER

Seniors, like lawyers, are the brunt of countless jokes. Despite the stories, I'm convinced that they're making adults younger these days. And they're making seniors younger too.

This is a favorable development for leaders who want to keep the turnover rate low, who want to fully utilize the talents of experienced people, and who want to take advantage of customer goodwill that has been developed over many years.

More and more workers are remaining in the workforce after age 65, a trend that began in the mid-1980s.

- - - - - Robert L. Bailey - - - - -

In 1950, 46% of men 65 and older were in the workforce. This percentage dropped to 16% by 1985 as the trend toward early retirement grew. Then the trend reversed. Now the 65ers have grown to 20% of the workforce with more rapid growth anticipated in the future.

AARP research shows that 77% of workers do not plan to retire at age 65. Merrill Lynch research was similar, with 76% saying they would continue to work—but 56% said they would work a different type of job. Gallup-UBS says 89% will continue to work, at least part time.

The trend is fueled by a number of factors, headed by three major categories—health, financial needs, and sense of purpose.

Health – There is strong evidence that people who work beyond 65 are healthier and live longer. Dr. Jochanan Stessman's research shows that there is a direct link between work and health and longevity.

Research by the University of Michigan and National Taiwan University shows that 100 hours of work per year is all it takes, leaving plenty of time for leisure pursuits. Those working for pay, their research continues, are only half as likely as non-workers to have bad health or die.

Why? Work forces us to have social contact, mental stimulation, and physical exercise, all of which promote physical and mental health and longevity.

Financial needs - It won't be a surprise when I tell you that it costs a lot to live. And it costs a lot to retire, too—more than most people can imagine.

When I learned that one of the employees of my former company planned to retire, I asked, *"Do you remember how much money you were making 35 or 40 years ago, when you joined the company?"*

Most could tell me almost precisely their salaries at that time—often in the $3,500 or $4,000 per year range.

"If I had offered you an opportunity to retire with 100% of your salary at that time, would you have taken it?" I continued.

"You bet I would. I would have jumped at it," most replied.

"How well would you be living today had you retired with 100% of your salary back then?" I would then ask.

The response: A look of concern—maybe shock.

"I don't know what will happen to our economy over the next 30 or 40 years," I continued, *"but it's reasonable to assume that the same set of economic conditions that have existed over the last 30 or 40 years will be repeated over the next 30 or 40 years. There will be high inflation years and low inflation years, but over the long pull, the economy will generally repeat itself.*

"If you can imagine what it would be like to live today on your salary 30 or 40 years ago, then try to imagine what it might be like living on today's retirement income over the next 30 or 40 years—a period over which you may well live."

I've found that most people approaching retirement haven't given enough thought to the financial demands that retirement will bring. It's also a fact that most people have not accumulated enough wealth to finance a comfortable retirement.

There are only a few alternatives to the financial constraints that retirement brings: (1) Die early (not an option I would recommend). (2) Work a few extra years and don't even think about early retirement. (3) Plan on a second career. (4) Brace yourself for some meager retirement years.

Sense of purpose – For some retirees, it's not concerns about money that hamper their retirement style. It's boredom. They need a purpose and a worthwhile mission beyond taking up space on this earth. They need to contribute to society. They need to remain connected to the real world.

Over the past several weeks I've met retirees—many of whom had served in responsible and well-paying jobs in business—who are actively involved in second careers. A retired airline pilot is working at a home improvement center. Another airline retiree is a waiter (and a darn good one). He agreed to "help out" a friend who owns a restaurant for a few days. He loved the interaction with people so much that he's still at it seven years later.

My wife visited with a supermarket bagger whose pension income is greater than the salary of the store manager—"*but I had to get out of the house and associate with real people,"* he said.

Not long ago I was the only passenger in a rental car van, driven by a man who appeared to be in his late 50s or early 60s. I struck up a conversation and learned that he had retired from a well-known local company, traveled extensively for two or three months and gotten that out of his system, pursued his *"honey do"* list and watched TV for another six months, *"and I started to go out of my mind,"* he said. *"So I took this job driving a rental car van about six months ago."*

"How do you like it?" I asked.

"I like it a lot. I meet a lot of interesting people," he answered.

"Did you ever meet any interesting people on your old job?" I continued.

"I don't know. I never thought about it."

One of the dimensions of your role as a leader is to help people find challenge and stimulation in their jobs and to help them build personal relationships that they can value through the years. If you accomplish this as a leader, your employees will make

106

even greater contributions to your company and will not see the need to count the days until retirement.

Everyone wants to be a part of a winning team. Everyone needs a worthwhile mission. Everyone wants to know what's going on in the industry and the company. Everyone wants to know what the competition is up to, what challenges the company faces and the plans to meet those challenges. Everyone wants to be able to make significant contributions to the success of the company.

Another dimension of leadership is to help people build a retirement nest egg to finance a comfortable retirement by participating in 401(k) and other voluntary retirement plans. It shouldn't be a surprise that Social Security will not pay for a life of luxury and leisure. I often told employees of my former company, "If you're not smart enough to participate in our 401(k) plan, you're not smart enough to work here." Still, about 15% did not participate.

Most people do not retire to get away from a job. They retire to get away from a poor leader. Therefore, it's critical that new leaders like you commit to building excellent leadership skills.

You are capable of building a team of dedicated people who remain stimulated and challenged throughout their careers. They do not count the days to retirement. What's even more important, this team, spiced with the judgment and experience of mature workers, can virtually guarantee the success of your business.

14

MAKE EVERY DAY A GREAT DAY

As the leader, you will have a lot on your plate—every day. As the leader, there are not many shoulders to cry on. You will find that it is indeed lonesome at the top.

There will be days when problems emerge from every source imaginable—people problems, customer problems, government problems, software problems. When you arrive home from work, family problems are added to your burden. At times you may ask, *"Why did I get into leadership? Isn't there an easier way to make a living?"*

Yes, there are probably many easier ways to make a living. But there are few ways that can be more rewarding and fulfilling.

Great leaders are upbeat!
Positive! Optimistic!

Furthermore, your people will expect you to be upbeat, positive and optimistic, and it's to your advantage to be so. Research has shown that optimists live longer than pessimists, have fewer heart attacks, and experience less pain. From personal experience I can assure you that, when you're an optimist, life is a lot more fun.

You can develop the characteristics of optimism just as you develop other skills. You can learn to get up when you're knocked down, brush yourself off, smile, and continue your mission. Falling down periodically is a part of life. None of us would have learned to walk had we not fallen down time and again.

Learn to love the challenges of business. These are simply hurdles that keep life interesting and free of boredom.

Learn to give those around you a much-needed lift. People feel better when they're around an optimistic leader. People have confidence they can solve any problem when their leader has confidence in them. Try to sense when a person needs a pat on the back or a gentle nudge.

- - - - - THE NEW LEADER - - - - -

Learn to take what life dishes out. Stand up for what you believe and let the blows and barbs glance off like cotton balls. Be tough. Leaders have to be tough when there are so many wussy, weak and whiny individuals who delight in pulling leaders down to their level.

Do leaders have bad days from time to time? Of course they do. But great leaders don't let it show.

Here are some things I have done throughout my business career which help to make every day a great day:

Act positive. Act like today is a great day. It won't be long until you won't have to act— the day really is a great day.

It's not hard to act once you recognize that there's value in everything that happens. Although elusive at times, when you look back, the value becomes apparent in the event that once seemed so devastating.

Tommy Lasorda of Los Angeles Dodgers fame said the most important thing he could do was *"walk into the clubhouse the right way. It didn't matter whether we had won eight in a row or lost eight in a row. The minute I came in, my players had to see an upbeat, positive manager. I had to walk straight, have a smile on my face and an optimistic gleam in my eye. If my players had seen my chin at my belt buckle, the gloom would have spread like wildfire."*

Our daughter, Nancy, had graduated from college and was looking for a job. She interviewed with a company in which she was particularly interested. "This is where I want to work," she insisted. "And the interviews went great. I liked them and they liked me. I just know they will offer me a job."

Several days later she was notified that another candidate had been selected.

When I arrived home from work, we went for a long walk. *"Nancy, I can't prove it to you today, but some day I will. I will prove to you that it is to your advantage that you were not offered this job,"* I said.

About two months later I phoned her and reminded her of our conversation. "I just learned that the office at which she had applied had been closed and every employee had been laid off."

Read something inspirational every day. The writings of Norman Vincent Peale are among my favorites. His books, *The Power of Positive Thinking* and others, remind me to be confident and relaxed as I go about solving the problems inherent in life and in any business. There is a solution to every problem. And most things we worry about never happen.

In my personal library there are three shelves devoted to books inspirational in nature. I prefer to read a chapter just before bedtime so that positive thoughts can permeate my mind during the night.

Another favorite publication is entitled *Plus*, published quarterly by the Outreach Division of *Guideposts* magazine.

And I shouldn't overlook *Guideposts*, which bills itself as "*True stories of hope and inspiration.*" When I read the stories in *Guideposts*, often by people who have overcome overwhelming problems and have gone on to achieve so much in life, I recognize just how manageable my problems are. If these folks can handle such big problems, then certainly my little problem can't possibly be a big deal.

And I shouldn't overlook *The Bible*, the greatest book of inspiration of all times.

Get some rest. I have found that problems are smaller and can be digested more easily when I am rested. When I arrive home at 1:00 a.m. after a late flight and the starting gun goes off at the usual 5:00 a.m., the problems that emerge during the day are bigger.

After a good night's sleep, the problem that seemed so weighty the day before doesn't seem so big. The solution is more readily apparent.

So I cut out the TV time and whenever possible go to bed early. It is said that optimists get up early; pessimists get up late. I think they're onto something.

Build a positive, capable team. None of us—even the most capable of leaders—can carry every burden alone. A great team can solve any problem.

Back in my corporate life, when asked why I did not appear to be worried about an unusually difficult problem, I often answered that I had a little book that provided answers to any conceivable problem. It's the company telephone directory. I could call a number in that little book and get the answer to nearly any question conceivable to mankind.

The people listed in that little booklet knew more about any one phase of the company or our industry than I could possibly know. The accountants knew more about accounting than I did; the underwriters knew more about underwriting than I did; the computer people knew more about computers than I did (the world's greatest understatement); the claims people knew more about claims handling than I did. And so it went throughout the company.

This positive, talented team used the *"Count to Ten"* technique to come up with solutions to problems. If we could think of ten alternatives, one was certain to stand out as the most acceptable approach.

Once the task was assigned to a certain individual, I simply made a note in a notebook: "The XYZ matter – John Jones – current date." This reminded me to follow up with John in a few days if I had not heard that the matter was resolved.

I learned through the years who the folks were who would follow through—thoroughly, effectively, every time—and those who had to be nudged periodically. The ones whom I could trust to complete the assignment without question emerged as the senior people in our organization. They lightened my load so that I could apply my time and attention to other emerging problems.

These positive people kept the environment positive and fun. We worked hard and we laughed hard. We learned that we must not take ourselves too seriously. The words humor and humility are rooted in the same Greek word.

When positive people are working in a positive environment, there is electricity in the air. It's fun to work in an environment like this. And when people are having fun, success is nearly guaranteed. A person who hates to go to work tomorrow will not be successful. And an unhappy employee will never treat your customers the way you want your customers to be treated.

Act positive. Read something inspirational every day. Get plenty of rest. And build a team of capable, positive people. When you do this, you'll find that you can have a great day every day. Guaranteed.

15

CONTROL YOUR EGO

It's desirable to have confidence in your abilities. You should have healthy self esteem. But confidence and self-worth can inflate to such an extreme that a bloated ego results.

Throughout my business career I have observed hundreds of leaders in action. Leaders who are most successful have not permitted their egos to get in the way. Truly important people don't have to act important. Some of the most important and richest people I have ever met are ordinary, sensible, down to earth folks who show greater interest in others than in themselves.

Even though your role in your organization is important, your spouse and kids won't be impressed. Your employees will be impressed even less. Nobody else cares. Come on back to earth and let your caring personality shine through.

"People don't leave companies; they leave their managers," a reader of my magazine column emailed. He hit the nail on the head. Poor leadership and inflated egos cause most employee turnover. Poor leadership and inflated egos can even cause physical illnesses. The ramifications of poor leadership are endless.

There's simply nothing that difficult about putting to work the skills required to be an outstanding leader.

First the don'ts:

Don't be a leader who, like royalty, talks down to direct reports—"This is what you do, like it or not, and if you don't do it you're fired. The era of the imperial boss is over.

Don't be a leader who takes advantage of extravagant perks, especially during periods of layoffs and other cost-cutting initiatives.

Don't be a leader who fails to set a positive example.

Don't be a leader who is not open or communicative or who never seeks the suggestions of those who have the best understanding of the problems and possible solutions—the people who actually do the work.

Don't be a leader who never expresses thanks or appreciation, even for truly outstanding performance. This applies to major projects as well as smaller but constructive missions that should be recognized.

Don't be a leader who seldom smiles or speaks to those within his or her jurisdiction.

It's time to do the things every leader knows how to do—use the skills that will reduce turnover, create a customer-focused culture, produce excellent results, and assure a healthy future.

Here's what to do:

Be a great communicator. Talk to people about the company, its problems, potential solutions, the competition, everything. They want to know. They want to be a part of a worthwhile mission. Every dimension of leadership always requires outstanding communication.

Be visible to employees at all levels. And be accessible. This energizes and motivates the organization.

Follow the same rules as everyone else. Make your own calls; take your own calls; observe standard work hours (and more); fly coach; park in the same parking lot; and eat in the same company cafeteria. People follow leaders who follow the rules.

Be a great coach and teacher. Continually seek ways to help the team learn and grow and serve customers better.

Be enthusiastic—a cheerleader of sorts. The last four letters of the word enthusiasm—IASM—mean I am sold myself. A leader who is not sold on the company, its products and services, and its mission, is in the wrong job—and probably in the wrong company.

Smile and greet people by name. There can be no communication without trust; and there can be no trust without a smile.

Take an interest in people and their families. After all, families take precedence over the company, and that's as it should be. If the happiness and satisfaction of your people and their families are ignored, you can't expect employees to go the extra mile for their employer.

Know the difference between right and wrong. And always do the right thing. I've asked hundreds of new employees of my former company if they know what it means to do the right thing, and I found that most people know. It's just common sense. Not only should you always do the right thing, but your people should be encouraged to do the same. If any situation in which you and your people are involved is accurately reported on the front page of your local newspaper or *USA Today* tomorrow morning, will most people read about the incident and say, "I think they did the right thing." That's the type of behavior that should be encouraged.

Understand your business, the services or products it provides, and the needs of customers you are serving. And keep learning, for conditions change rapidly. If you don't understand the big picture, the small picture will get out of focus.

If you're worried (and you will be on occasion), don't let it show. Be confident—in your own abilities and those of your team. Most things you worry about never happen.

Have a burning desire to make your organization a winner—to help it serve customers in the most efficient and effective way possible. Put your company before yourself. Over the long pull, people succeed only when organizations succeed.

There's nothing difficult about the leadership techniques described in this book. Just keep at it and over time a winning leadership style will become a way of life—a way of life your people will like—a way of life that will produce a highly motivated, happy, productive, effective and stable workforce— the kind of workforce that builds successful companies.

This is also a way of life that produces successful families. Great leadership on the job is the same form of leadership that is appropriate wherever people work together—at home, school, church, or community organizations.

Commit yourself to being an outstanding leader every day.

THE AUTHOR

The author often refers to himself as "self-unemployed." But since his retirement in 2000, he is far from unemployed. He is the retired CEO, President and Chairman of the State Auto Insurance Companies, is the author of the books *Plain Talk About Leadership* (Franklin University Press – 2002) and What *Do You Do When You're Having a Bad Day?* (Peppertree Press – 2008), and is a columnist for *Rough Notes* magazine. He has a rather intense schedule as a professional public speaker. These activities produce a work schedule that would challenge most people half his age.

Under his leadership of the State Auto Insurance Companies since 1983, the company became one of the top performing property and casualty insurance companies in the United States. Several companies were added to the State Auto Group (now 13 insurance companies and several other subsidiary companies), the company entered 13 additional states, and the Company became publicly owned in 1991 with the formation of State Auto Financial Corporation.

Since the Financial Corporation's first full year as a public corporation through his retirement at yearend 2000, compound average annual growth rates were: revenues 14%; earnings per share 23%; equity 14%; assets 17%; and book value per share 16%. From 1991 through 1997, State Auto stock was the 85th best performer on the NASDAQ exchange.

Under his leadership, sales rose from $214 million to more than $1 billion, net worth increased from $129 million to nearly $1 billion, and service levels were improved dramatically under what he calls an "overwhelming service" objective. At the same time employee morale rose to the highest level ever, thanks to a strong focus on communication, recognition and motivation. The accomplishments of the Companies have been noted in publications by Tom Peters, co-author of the best selling books on business management, In Search of Excellence, A Passion for Excellence, and others.

He entered the insurance business in 1958 with the Western Casualty and Surety Company of Fort Scott, Kansas (now a part of the Safeco Group)—near the farm where he was raised and where he attended a one-room country school. He is quick to point out that for six of the eight years of elementary school he was the top student in class. After a few seconds hesitation, he adds, "I was also the bottom student in class—I was the only one."

He is a graduate of Pittsburg (Kansas) State University following two years at Fort Scott (Kansas) Community College. In 2001 FSCC named him its outstanding alumnus. Pittsburg State University awarded him its Meritorious Achievement Award in 2007, the highest honor Pitt State bestows on its alumni. In 2000 the Professional Insurance Agents Association named him the Insurance Industry Person of the Year. Franklin University, where he served as chairman and a board member for many years, awarded him an honorary doctorate degree in 2006. In response to a number of honors he has received through the years, he says, "I think I've got this figured out. They do this alphabetically. It took them 50 years to get to the Bs. If your name is Smith or Wilson, you don't have a chance."

He holds the Chartered Property and Casualty Underwriter (CPCU) designation, the equivalent of CPA in accounting, and is an Associate in Risk Management.

As one might expect for a person with his executive talent, he has served on, and has been chairman of, a long list of community and industry boards. He is a member of the National Speakers Association, the Sarasota (Florida) Chamber of Commerce, and the Sarasota Baptist Church.

Bob Bailey, a dynamic person with a great sense of humor, understands what it takes to become a truly great leader.

Julie Ann Howell
Peppertree Press

OTHER BOOKS
BY
ROBERT L. BAILEY

Plain Talk About Leadership
Franklin University Press

**What Do You Do
When You're Having a Bad Day?**
Peppertree Press